ORIGINAL CORNMEAL COOKBOOK

Cornmeal at its Finest

By

Ema Skooh

FM Publishing Company
Atlanta, GA 30302

Original Cornmeal Cookbook

Cornmeal at its Finest

Published by:

FM Publishing Company
P.O. Box 4211
Atlanta, GA 30302
United States of America
www.fmpublishingcompany.com

Printed in the United States of America
ISBN 9781931671361
Library of Congress Control Number 2011934191

Photography by Linda Tawney Portrait Studio

Dedication

This, my first recipe book, is dedicated to my eight brothers and two sisters who shared every meal possible with me - as it was the mealtime custom that we all break bread - yes, cornbread together, at least two of the three meals each day, 365 days a year.

Whenever possible, Papa (who often worked away from home) would sit at the "head" of this long, long wooden table and my mother sat at the "foot." There were two long, long wooden benches - one on either side of the table with an assigned space for each of us to sit. Of course, our parents sat in chairs, in fact, the only two good chairs in our house except in their room.

I asked Papa why he always sat at the head of the table and Mom had to sit at the foot. He replied: "From where I sit, I can see the door and protect you if someone comes in that shouldn't and your mother sits at the foot which is closer to the stove. She can give you a second helping of food if you want more."

Special thanks are in order to my parents for their love and guidance. To my sister, Margaret, whose opinion I truly value, and especially to Bill Hall for his support and encouragement from my first recipe.

My publisher, editor, and photographer were instrumental in making my work easier through their advice and support.

For my children and their families

Foreword & Acknowledgement

I was fortunate enough to be contacted by Ema Skooh when she began working on her cornmeal cookbook. She is a wonderful woman with incredible spirit and reminded me of all the delicious foods I had as a child that had been prepared with cornmeal. I miss the hot-water cornbread that my great-grandmother used to make with cornmeal. I can still remember the aroma in the kitchen as she prepared it.

It wasn't until I began work with Native Seeds/SEARCH here in Tucson that I came in contact with cornmeal again and have been lucky enough to enjoy many meals that include various types of cornmeal products. Native Seeds/SEARCH has a large selection of corn seeds to be planted as well as cornmeal products in our store which are used by our customers all over the United States and can be used for the recipes which are in this cookbook.

Ema Skooh's *The Original Cornmeal Cookbook* will be a great addition to anyone's cookbook collection especially those who want to try some of the tried and true southern tastes. In fact I would encourage everyone to sometimes mix in a little bit of our southwest flavors to give that extra zest.

Happy cooking and eating!!

JP Wilhite
Director of Distribution
Native Seeds/SEARCH
Tucson, AZ

Table of Contents

Introduction

Corn was the most important commodity in my family's world. There was never a day without it playing a dominant role in our lives. It seems that we were always planting, tilling, pulling, storing, and shucking corn to take to the grist mill for cornmeal and grits. Numerous pounds were used as food for us and feed for our farm animals.

Corn was the ultimate staple in our lives as it not only provided the cornmeal, but was viable as a vegetable and a cereal in our diet. Research shows corn as a fruit produced from a grass and not a vegetable. It is indigenous to Central America. Only about 1 in every 100 ears of corn produced in the United States is eaten by people.

As a child growing up in Tuskegee, Alabama in the community of Milstead, I knew only four kinds of breads – namely, biscuits for breakfast that were made by hand 365 days a year and light bread which is produced in a commercial baker. Today, we recognize it as a "loaf of bread." This is so taken for granted today, but to us, it was really a special treat. The smell of the yeast and the perfect texture of the soft slice put a smile on my face as I bit into it. Yeast rolls were a novelty and were rarely served. But, old faithful – **corn bread** was there once a day – all day long. I do not remember a time when we were out of cornmeal. Nor do I remember a time that there was not the smell of hot cornbread when we walked in from school or from the field.

With eight sons and three daughters to feed, my parents knew the value of keeping us happy. Papa would say, "You can go a long way on a full belly." In other words, you can pick a lot of cotton or pull a lot of corn now that you have been fed well. And fed well we were.

Introduction (cont'd)

Two things my mom did daily: bake biscuits for breakfast and cornbread for dinner and supper – no exception. In addition to baking cornbread, she would sometimes treat us with some fried bread we called flap jacks or a hoecake. Now if you think cornbread is good, you should try the flapjacks. They are delicious, especially when eaten hot with syrup, fresh butter, and a glass of cold milk. All of the fish we ate, which was very often since we lived at the creek, were battered in cornmeal before frying, as was okra, green tomatoes, and eggplants.

Mom would make cornmeal dumplings and put them in our vegetables. That is what I called a one-pot meal. When you dipped up the greens, the starch and meat were there. The taste is unforgettable.

It was not until Mom had to go out of town (which was very seldom) for an emergency that I realized that cornmeal could be used for other than cornbread. Papa had to prepare dinner for us that first night. I could not believe that he made *cornmeal gravy* for serving with our mashed white potatoes. It was truly a major revelation to me. That is when my mind started to wonder (at about age 5), how else could cornmeal be used in food preparation. At the age of 30, I experimented with battering chicken in cornmeal for frying just as we had for fish. Good job. Some years later, I rolled chicken in cornmeal batter and baked it. It turned out wonderful. Well, needless to say, until recently, August 2010, I had taken no interest in exploring my curiosity about cornmeal cuisine until after I had an epiphany while asleep one morning. I bolted from the bed and began this cornmeal quest.

Introduction (cont'd)

I established a test kitchen and began experimenting and creating other recipes. My first recipe was cornmeal mush. Shortly thereafter, I added cornmeal gravy for the finishing touch. Cornmeal gravy brings new life to the solitary pork chops or grilled, open-face turkey sandwich or potatoes of any color.

So far, I have written, researched and collected many recipes, of which only a few are represented here in this, my first cookbook.

It is my passion to write a larger cookbook to include all of my recipes and to add more through research which will include more cornmeal beverages.

The corn whiskey and baked rattle snake were not tried nor tested. Prepare and eat at your own risk; **this is offered merely as entertainment.

BREADS

Blue Cornbread

Blue Cornbread

Set oven at 350 degrees Fahrenheit.   8 ½ x 4 ½ loaf pan

Ingredients:

Blue Cornmeal	½ cup
Flour, all purpose	½ cup
Baking powder	2 teaspoons
Sugar	1/8 cup
Salt	½ teaspoon
Egg, well beaten	1
Butter, soft	¼ cup (add more if you like richer bread)
Milk	¾ cup

Directions:

In a mixing bowl, mix all of the dry ingredients together. Gradually add egg, milk and butter. Stir well and bake in two 3-inch round well greased baking tins sprinkled with cornmeal as a releasing agent and bake for 30 minutes or until fully cooked. When done, remove and set aside for a few minutes before removing from pan.

Blue Cornbread – Yeast

Set oven at 350 degrees Fahrenheit

Baking utensils: Four 3x5 size loaf pans

Ingredients:

Dry yeast, packet	1	Water	1 cup, warm
Water (room temperature)	½ cup	Egg	1 large
Cornmeal, blue	1 ¼ cup	Flour	1 ½ cup
Butter, soft	1/3 cup	Salt	1 teaspoon
Sugar	4 tablespoons		

Directions: Mix all dry ingredients in a mixing bowl. Beat yeast, water, egg, and butter together. Add to dry ingredients. Let dough rise to double in size. Punch down by stirring. Let rise to double in size again. Stir dough vigorously and pour about 6 ounces of dough in each of the loaf pans and let it stand at room temperature until the dough rises to near even with top of pan. Place in hot oven for 25-30 minutes. Remove and let set for 4 minutes. Take out of pan and serve hot. Excellent served with soup.

Cornbread Chomps

Cornbread Chomps

Set oven at 375 degrees Fahrenheit

Ingredients:

Cornmeal	1 cup
Flour	1 cup
Sugar	1/3 cup
Salt	1 teaspoon
Baking powder	1 teaspoon
Baking soda	½ teaspoon
Ginger & nutmeg	¼ teaspoon
Buttermilk	1 cup
Butter or vegetable oil	¼ cup
Corn, whole kernel canned or frozen	½ cup

Directions:

Mix all dry ingredients a bowl. Add remainder ingredients being sure that the eggs are well beaten until fluffy. Pour batter into a well greased baking dish and bake for 25 minutes or until golden brown. Remove from oven and serve as a snack or with conventional meal.

Cornbread Dressing

Cornbread Dressing

Preheat oven to 375° F. Grease a 7x3 inch baking dish and sprinkle with meal.

Ingredients:

Cornbread crumbled	2 cups packed
Sliced bread, crumbled	3
Egg, well beaten	1
Milk	1 cup
Butter, room temperature	¼ cup
Sugar	2 tablespoons
Chicken broth	1- 14.5 oz can
Onion, medium finely chopped	1
Celery, finely chopped	1/3 cup
Sage	2 teaspoons
Poultry Seasoning	1 teaspoon
Black pepper	½ teaspoon
Salt	1/8 teaspoon

Directions:

In a mixing bowl, beat the egg well. Add the chicken broth and all of the other ingredients except the milk. Mix thoroughly and add the milk as needed. Let stand about 5 minutes and pour into a well greased baking dish (about 9 inches) that has been dusted with cornmeal as a releasing agent. Bake about 30 minutes at 375 degrees Fahrenheit or until brown.

Polenta Spinach Casserole

Polenta Spinach Casserole

Preheat oven to 350 degrees Fahrenheit

Ingredients:

Polenta, finely ground	¾ cup
Water (used to moisten polenta)	½ cup
Spinach, frozen chopped	1 box
Let thaw, drain and add spinach liquid to Water for	2½ cups
Olives (your choice) diced	½ cup
Garlic, minced	1 tablespoon
Cheese, Sharp grated	¼ cup
Olive Oil	¼ cup
Salt	1/8 teaspoon
Sugar	1 tablespoon

Directions:

In a bowl, moisten the polenta with the ½ cup of water. In a large skillet, place olive oil, add spinach, garlic, a pinch of salt, olives, and a pinch of sugar. Sauté on medium heat for 12 minutes. In a pot, bring to boil the water and vigorously stir in the moistened polenta. Mix all of the ingredients together. Pour into a 6-cup well greased baking dish that is sprinkled with cornmeal as a releasing agent.

Cover the casserole with the cheese sauce topping (p. 20) and place under the broiler at 350° Fahrenheit and cook about 10 minutes or until nice and bubbly.

Polenta Spinach Casserole (cont'd)

Cheese sauce toppings
Ingredients:

Olive Oil	2 tablespoons
Cheese, Sharp grated	½ cup
Canned milk	½ cup
Pinch of black pepper	
Pinch of salt	
Pinch of sugar	
Pinch of red pepper	

Directions: Mix well and sprinkle over casserole.

Open Face Turkey Waffle Sandwich

Open Face Turkey Waffle Sandwich

Put 2 ½ oz. sliced or chopped warm turkey on a cornmeal waffle and smother in cornmeal gravy.

Cooking Time: Quick lunch

Preheat oven to 350° Fahrenheit

Ingredients:

Turkey	2½ oz. Sliced or chop up turkey
Cornmeal, white	¼ cup
Butter	2 tablespoons
Onion, coarsely chopped	1 small
Mushroom, sliced small	1
Boiling Water	2 cups

Spices: a pinch of black pepper, sage, thyme, garlic, parsley and sugar.

Directions:

In a skillet, place the butter and cornmeal. Cook while stirring until cornmeal is just brown. Take off heat. Add onions, mushrooms spices and a tablespoon of diced turkey pieces. Sir well. Carefully pour the boiling water over the fried cornmeal mix for a tasty sauce, set the mixture aside, covered.

Cornmeal gravy

Cornmeal, white	¼ cup	All-Purpose flour		¼ cup	
Salt	¼ teaspoon	Baking powder		1 teaspoons	
Sugar	2 tablespoons	Pecan chips		¼ cup	
Butter	2 tablespoons	Egg, beaten		1 (room tem)	
Milk more or less as needed		½ cup			

Directions:

In a mixing bowl, add all dry ingredients, add a little milk at a time, butter and egg, a tablespoon of chopped turkey and more milk until batter is thin enough for the waffle iron. Sometimes, it is hard to have the exact amount of batter, so be careful that you don't overfill the waffle iron.

Salmon Stuffed Red Pepper

Salmon Stuffed Red Pepper

Cooking Time: 30-40 minutes

Preheat oven to 350°

Ingredients:

Salmon, can	7 ½ oz.	Cornmeal	1/8 cup
Red Bell Pepper	1	Onion, chopped	2
Mushroom, small, chopped	1	Pepper. Red/black	pinch
Garlic, minced	1/8 teaspoon	Salt	pinch
Honey	1/8 teaspoon	Egg, well beaten	1
Butter, melted	2 tablespoon		
Old Bay Seasoning	1/8 teaspoon		

Directions:

Core and remove the interior of the pepper. Take a long handle brush and brush the inside of the pepper with butter. Pour all unused butter into mixing bowl. Finely chop the scraps of pepper into the mixing bowl.

Place all of the ingredients into the mixing bowl and stir well. Use same brush for the butter and wipe over the pepper. Pack the pepper. Put pepper(s) into a well-greased baking dish and bake for about 35 minutes. Remove from oven and let cool.

Ground Beef Stuffed Pepper

Ground Beef Stuffed Peppers

Red, Orange or Yellow. Mixture will fill 2 peppers.

Cooking Time: 50 minutes

Preheat oven to 350° Fahrenheit

Ingredients:

Ground Beef	4 ounces	Cornmeal	1 tablespoon
Bell Pepper	2	Onion, chopped	1 tablespoon
Rice, partial pre-cooked	1/4 cup	Pepper, Red/black, pinch	
Garlic, minced	1/8 teaspoon	Salt, pinch	
Sugar	1/8 teaspoon	Tomato, chopped	1
Celery chopped very fine	1 tablespoon	Seasoning Salt	1 teaspoon
Worcestershire sauce	2 dashes		

Directions:

Wash and hew out the inside of two peppers, and using a long handled brush, coat the inside and outside of the peppers with olive oil or vegetable oil. Use the inners removed from the peppers in the mixture for seasoning. Carefully pack each pepper. Place in a compact, well greased baking dish and bake for about 50 minutes.

Remove from oven and let cool.

Black-Eyed Pea Casserole

Black-Eyed Pea Casserole

Cooking Time: 55 minutes

Preheat oven to 350°

Ingredients (Part 1):

Bacon	4 strips	Cornmeal	½ cup
Flour-all purpose	½ cup	Sugar	2 tablespoons
Salt (optional	1 teaspoon	Baking powder	2 teaspoon
Egg, beaten	1	Milk	
Oil or butter	2 tablespoons		

Directions:

Fry enough bacon to generate 3 ounces of crumbled bits – set aside

Save bacon grease to mix in batter.

Place all dry ingredients together in a bowl and mix with the egg and oil, add milk as needed.

Black-Eyed Pea Casserole (cont'd)

Ingredients (Part 2):

Water	4½ cups	Salt	1 teaspoon
Black eye peas frozen	12 ounces	Butter	3 tablespoon
Carrot, chopped small	½ cup	Tomato	2 small
Okra, chopped small	¼ cup	Onion	1 small

Prepare vegetables in advance and set aside until the peas have boiled for 20 minutes. Add in the additional vegetables with the peas, stirring constantly. Bring the pot back to a boil and add the cornbread batter and ½ the beacon bits. Mix the batter and the vegetables well; pour into baking dish to accommodate the food or separate and bake smaller portions.

Sprinkle the remainder of bacon bits over the top and bake at 350° Fahrenheit for about 55 minutes or until done.

DESSERTS

Strawberry Pudding Cake

Strawberry Pudding Cake

Cooking Time: 30-40 minutes

Preheat oven to 375°

Ingredients:

Red cornmeal	I cup	Flour	¾ cup
Sugar	I cup	Sugar	1/8 cup
Salt	I teaspoon	Milk	I Cup
Baking powder	I teaspoon	Egg	I
Nutmeg & Allspice	1/8 teaspoon	Vanilla flavor	I tablespoon
Vanilla pudding	I cup	Butter	4 tablespoons
Cool Whip	I 8oz can	Strawberries	I cup

Cut into quarters and sprinkled with small amount of sugar

Directions: Slice strawberries in half and place in a small dish and sprinkle with a teaspoon of sugar. Let stand, covered. In a mixing bowl, cream the butter, sugar and egg together. Add milk and mix well. Gradually add all of the dry ingredients and thoroughly mix. Fold in the vanilla pudding mix, sliced strawberries and stir gently. Pour the batter into a well greased 6x6x2 inch baking dish that has been sprinkled with cornmeal as a releasing agent. Bake for 30-40 minutes. Remove from oven and cool. After about 45 minutes, cover the pudding cake with Cool Whip and garnish with sliced strawberries.

Coconut Cornmeal Pudding

Coconut Cornmeal Pudding

Cooking Time: 35 minutes

Preheat oven to 350° Fahrenheit

Ingredients:

Yellow Cornmeal	1 ½ cup	Flour	1½ cup
Sugar - Brown	1-1/8 cup	Sugar-White	1/8 cup
Salt	1 teaspoon	Butter	1 cup
Baking powder	2 teaspoons	Egg	2
Nutmeg	1 teaspoon	Allspice	½ teaspoon
Cream Corn	½ cup		
Coconut, shredded	¼ cup	Coconut milk	1 ½ cup
Raisins	½ cup	Rum	¼ cup

Snip raisins into small pieces with scissors and soak in rum over night.

Directions:

Place eggs, butter, sugar, and coconut milk in a mixing bowl and mix well. Stir in corn and rum/raisins. Gradually add the dry ingredients as you go, alternating with the coconut milk. Pour into a 10-inch round well greased baking dish that has been sprinkled with cornmeal as a releasing agent. Bake for 30 minutes.

Coconut Cornmeal Pudding (cont'd)

Sauce Mixture—Ingredients:

Coconut milk, Strong	¼ cup
Sugar, White granulated	4 tablespoons
Cinnamon	smidgen
Salt	pinch
Vanilla flavor	½ teaspoon
Rum flavor	½ teaspoon

Directions:

Combine all ingredients. Remove pudding from oven and pour sauce on top of pudding and continue to bake about 30 minutes more. Remove when coconut is brown.

Cornmeal Indian Pudding

Cornmeal Indian Pudding

Cooking Time: 2 hours

Preheat oven to 250° Fahrenheit

Ingredients:

Yellow Cornmeal	½ cup	Flour	½ cup
Milk	6 cups	Molasses	½ cup
Sugar - Brown	1/3 cup	Sugar-White	1/3 cup
Salt	1 teaspoon	Butter	½ cup
Baking powder	1/8 teaspoon	Egg	3
Nutmeg	1 teaspoon	Ginger	1 teaspoon
Cinnamon	1 teaspoon		

Directions: Mix all dry ingredients in a plastic bag and set aside. In a mixing bowl, sift all dry ingredient together and add molasses, eggs and 1 cup of cold milk. Place 3 cups of milk in a larger pot and heat to near boiling point, stirring constantly. Add the cornmeal mixture to the hot milk, and cook while stirring until it thickens. Add raisins. Pour into a 10-inch round well greased baking dish that has been sprinkled with cornmeal as a releasing agent. Bake for 2½ hours. Let stand for a few minutes if you plan to remove it from the baking dish.

Pear Muffins

Cooking Time: 40 minutes

Preheat oven to 400° Fahrenheit

Ingredients:

Polenta	½ cup	Flour	½ cup
Sugar-White	2 tablespoon	Salt	¼ teaspoon
Baking powder	2 teaspoon	Ginger	¼ teaspoon
Egg beaten	1	Pecan chips	¼ cup
Pear, quarters	3 thinly sliced	Pear Juice	¼ cup
Butter, melted	3 tablespoon	Vanilla Flavoring few drops	
Sweetened condensed milk	¼ cup		

Pear Muffins (cont'd)

Directions:

Mix all dry ingredient in a bowl. Mix beaten egg, condensed milk, butter pear juice, pear quarters, and Vanilla extract and add to dry ingredients. Blend in pecans. Place muffin liners in muffin pan and spoon fill each liner to top. Lower temp to 375° and bake for about 40 minutes or until brown to your satisfaction. Remove from heat.

Mix 2 tablespoons of butter with powdered sugar and a dash of nutmeg brushed over the top of muffins.

Makes 6 muffins

Apple Muffins

Ingredients:

Polenta	½ cup	Flour	½ cup
Sugar-White	2 tablespoon	Salt	¼ teaspoon
Baking powder	2 teaspoon	Ginger	¼ teaspoon
Clove	¼ teaspoon	Egg beaten	1
Pecan chips	¼ cup		

Apples, quarters, 3 thinly sliced   Apple Juice   ¼ cup

Butter, melted   3 tablespoon   Vanilla Flavoring few drops

Sweetened condensed milk   ¼ cup

Apple Muffins (cont'd)

Directions:

Mix all dry ingredient in a bowl. Mix beaten egg, condensed milk, butter, apple juice, apple quarters, and vanilla extract and add to dry ingredients. Blend in pecans. Place muffin liners in muffin pan and spoon fill each liner to top. Lower temp to 375° and bake for about 40 minutes or until brown to your satisfaction. Remove from heat.

Mix 2 tablespoons of butter with powdered sugar at room temperature and add a dash of ginger. Spread or brush over top of muffins while warm.

Red, White & Blue Cornbread Stack

Red Cornbread Stack

Preheat oven to 375° F. Grease a 3-inch baking dish and sprinkle with meal as a releasing agent.

Ingredients:

*Red Cornbread	I cup
Flour, all purpose	I cup
Egg, well beaten	I
Baking powder	2 teaspoons
Butter, soft	¼ cup
Sugar	1/3 cup
Salt	½ teaspoon
Ginger	1/8 teaspoon
Milk	2 cups (more or less)
*Red food color – gel-like	I mini drop

Directions:

Place all dry ingredients into a mixing bowl. Add egg, butter, and gradually add milk as you thoroughly blend the ingredients. Mix food color well. Pour about ½ cup batter into a 3-inch round baking dish and bake for 30 minutes or until done. Remove from the oven. Let it stand a few minutes before removing from the dish.

*After red corn meal is baked, it loses some of its redness. I recommend obtaining red gel-like food color from a cake baker's store or an arts and crafts store. Be cautious; it takes a minimum amount for this recipe.

White Cornbread Stack

Preheat oven to 375° F. Grease a 3-inch baking dish and sprinkle with meal as a releasing agent.

Ingredients:

White Cornbread	I cup
Flour, all purpose	I cup
Egg, well beaten	I
Baking powder	2 teaspoons
Butter, soft	¼ cup
Sugar	1/3 cup
Nutmeg	1/8 teaspoon
Salt	½ teaspoon
Baking Soda	I teaspoon
Buttermilk	2 cups

Directions:

Place all dry ingredients into a mixing bowl. Add egg, butter, and gradually add milk as you thoroughly blend the ingredients. Mix Use only the amount of milk necessary for the consistency you want. After blending, pour about ½ cup batter into a 3-inch round baking dish and bake for 30 minutes or until done. Remove from the oven. Let it stand a few minutes before removing from the dish.

Blue Cornbread Stack

Preheat oven to 375° F. Grease a 3-inch baking dish and sprinkle with meal as a releasing agent.

Ingredients:

*Blue Cornbread	1 cup
Flour, all purpose	1 cup
Egg, well beaten	1
Butter, soft	¼ cup
Sugar	1/3 cup
Salt	½ teaspoon
Allspice	1/8 teaspoon
Milk	2 cups
*Blue food color – gel-like	1 mini drop

Directions:

Place all dry ingredients into a mixing bowl. Add egg, butter, and gradually add milk as you thoroughly blend the ingredients. Mix food color well. Pour about ½ cup batter into a 3-inch round baking dish and bake for 30 minutes or until done. Remove from the oven. Let it stand a few minutes before removing from the dish.

Batter for stacking

Ingredients:

Butter, room temperature	1 stick
Honey	½ cup
All spice and cinnamon mixed	¼ teaspoon

Blend all ingredients and slather the honey butter between, around, and on top of bread stacks, and serve.

DRINKS

Atole– A Mexican Drink

This is a great drink for cool weather or for relaxing at bedtime.

Ingredients:

Milk or water	5 cups	Mesa harina	½ cup
Sugar	1/3 cup	Brown Sugar	½ cup
Cinnamon	½ teaspoon	Salt	1/8 teaspoon
Vanilla Flavoring	1 teaspoon	Nutmeg	¼ teaspoon

Atole– A Mexican Drink (cont'd)

Directions

1. Place all ingredients into a large saucepan and beat until smooth.

2. Place saucepan over medium heat and bring to a boil, stirring constantly.

3. Reduce heat to medium low and continue to stir for about 5 minutes or until mixture is thick enough for your satisfaction.

4. Remove from heat, stir in vanilla and serve hot in mugs.

Chocolate Atole

Serves 4

Ingredients:

Milk or water	5 cups	Mesa harina	½ cup
Sugar	1/3 cup	Brown Sugar	¼ cup
Cinnamon	½ teaspoon	Salt	¼ teaspoon
Vanilla Flavoring	1 teaspoon	Nutmeg	¼ teaspoon
Chocolate, chopped Mexican	4 oz.		

Chocolate Atole (cont'd)

Directions:

1. Place all ingredients, <u>except the vanilla and chocolate</u>, into a large saucepan and beat until smooth.

2. Place saucepan over medium heat and bring to a boil, stirring constantly.

3. Reduce heat to medium low and continue to stir for about 5 minutes or until mixture is thick enough for your satisfaction.

4. Remove from heat, stir in chocolate and vanilla. Stir until chocolate is completely dissolved. Whisk beverage briskly until frosty on top.

5. Best served hot in mugs.

Cornmeal Whiskey

Cornmeal Whiskey**

Equipment needed. Carboy and stove. Be sure the carboy is clean.

Ingredients:

Cornmeal, your choice	3 pounds
Malt, dark-dry (suggested)	1 ½ pound
Yeast	1 sachet of 48 turbo yeast
Spring Water	4 gallons

Directions:

Place 3½ gallons of water into the carboy and then slowly add the cornmeal allowing it to wet as it falls to the bottom in order to avoid caking as much as possible. Then carefully lift the carboy and shake it well to ensure a good mix. Next, add the dry malt with the same slow steady precision as you did the cornmeal. Again lift the carboy and shake it for a thorough mix.

With the leftover ½ gallon of water, heat it on the stove until it is just hot to the touch. Stir in the yeast until it is completely dissolved. Finally, add this yeast mixture to that in the carboy and shake vigorously. Let Stand.

After 3 to 7 days, it is now ready to run off in the still.

**Use at your own risk. This recipe has not been tested nor tasted. It has been included for you to use at your own risk. It is also added for your entertainment.

For Exotic Tastes

Rattlesnake

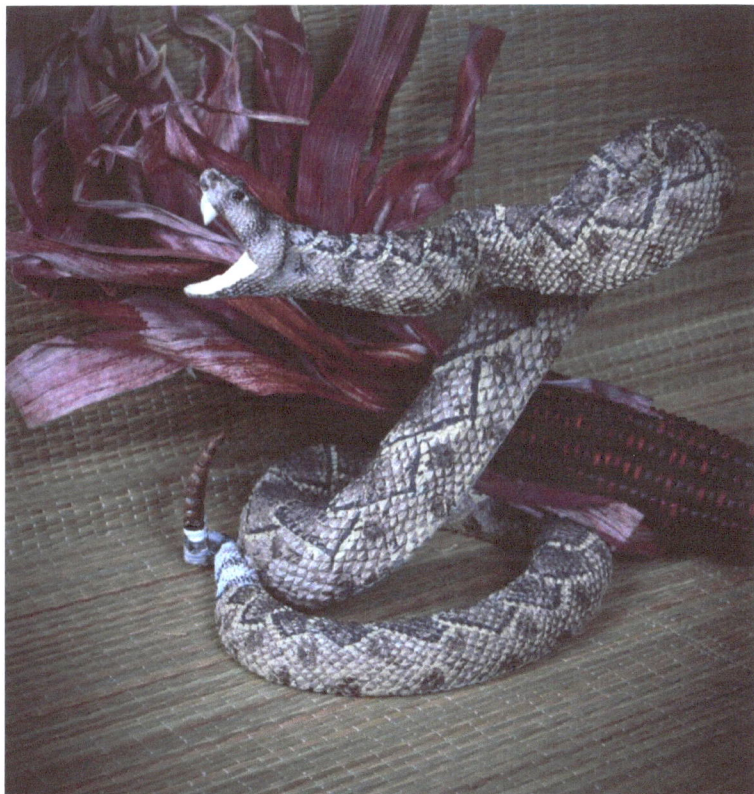

Rattlesnake**

Cooking Time: 30 minutes

Preheat oven to 350° Fahrenheit

Ingredients:

Rattlesnake filet ½ pound		Cornmeal	½ cup
Olive Oil	¼ cup	Lemon juice	¼ cup
Flour	¼ cup	oregano	1 tablespoon
Basil	1 tablespoon	Salt	¼ teaspoon
Black Pepper *	1 teaspoon	Red Pepper *	¼ teaspoon
Seasoning salt	¼ teaspoon		
Sugar	1 teaspoon		

*More hot peppers may be added to your taste.

**Prepare and eat at your own risk. This Recipe has not been tested nor tasted. It has been included for entertainment purposes only.

Rattlesnake** (cont'd)

Directions:

Pour the snake into a colander and let drain. Shake the strainer a bit to help the liquid drain. Mix all of the dry ingredients together in a plastic bag and set aside. Thoroughly mix the olive oil and lemon juice and 1 teaspoon of sugar together in a mixing bowl. Place the filet of snake in the oil mixtures until they are saturated. Remove them and drop into the plastic bag of dry ingredients and shake until each piece is thoroughly coated. Remove each piece of snake and place evenly in a medium depth baking pan. Add 2 ½ cups of water to the remainder of mixture in the plastic bag and pour over the snake. Cover and place in oven. After 30 minutes of serious cooking, reduce heat to 250° F and cook for another 30 minutes.

**Prepare and eat at your own risk. This Recipe has not been tested nor tasted. It has been included for entertainment purposes only.

Publication Ordering Information

Use **Order Form** on p. 58 or **order online** at:

www.amazon.com

www.createspace.com

www.fmpublishingcompany.com

www.lulu.com

www.gerilorraine.org/fmpubco

Phone: 877-392-3906

Email: fmpublishing@cox.net

Fax: 520-208-9786

Order Form

Please send to me _____ copies of Emma Skooh's
The Original Cornmeal Cookbook at a retail price of $14.95 each.

Shipping & Handling:

1 to 3 copies: Add $3.99

4 to 10 copies: Add $10.99

11 to 20 copies: Add $15.99

21 to 40 copies: Add $25.99

41 + copies: Add $30.99

Total Cost: $_____

Check/Money Order # _____

If ordering by credit card:

Card Type: _____

Card # _____

Expiration Date: _____   CVC: _____

Name of Card: _____

Ship order to:

Name:_____

Address:_____

City/State/Zip:_____

www.ingramcontent.com/pod-product-compliance
Lightning Source LLC
Chambersburg PA
CBHW040036110426
42741CB00031B/111